LIVING WITH SUBSTANCE ADDICTION

LIVING WITH SUBSTANCE ADDICTION

by Melissa Higgins

Content Consultant
Joseph W. Ditre, PhD, Clinical Psychologist and Assistant Professor of Psychology, Texas A&M University, College Station, TX

LIVING WITH HEALTH CHALLENGES

CREDITS

Published by ABDO Publishing Company, PO Box 398166, Minneapolis, MN 55439. Copyright © 2012 by Abdo Consulting Group, Inc. International copyrights reserved in all countries. No part of this book may be reproduced in any form without written permission from the publisher. The Essential Library™ is a trademark and logo of ABDO Publishing Company.

Printed in the United States of America, North Mankato, Minnesota
102011
012012

 THIS BOOK CONTAINS AT LEAST 10% RECYCLED MATERIALS.

Editor: Lisa Owings
Copy Editor: Karen Latchana Kenney
Series design and cover production: Becky Daum
Interior production: Kazuko Collins

Library of Congress Cataloging-in-Publication Data
Higgins, Melissa, 1953-
  Living with substance addiction / by Melissa Higgins.
      p. cm. -- (Living with health challenges)
  Includes bibliographical references.
  ISBN 978-1-61783-129-4
  1. Substance abuse--Juvenile literature. I. Title.
  RC564.3.H54 2012
  616.86--dc23
                              2011033157

TABLE OF CONTENTS

EXPERT ADVICE

Addiction is a difficult disease to live with, no matter how old you are. I am currently an assistant professor of psychology at Texas A&M University and have been studying addiction and associated disorders for eight years. I have also written extensively on the subject of nicotine addiction. As a teen, it may be especially hard for you to stay away from the people, places, and situations that trigger your cravings. If your family members are addicted or unwilling to support your treatment, it can also be hard to know where to turn for help. Here is my advice as you start down your road to recovery:

Get help wherever you can find it. Ask your family for support in getting treatment for your addiction. If a family member can't or won't help, talk to a teacher, a school counselor, or your doctor. No matter how severe your addiction is, remember that you are not alone. There are many people and organizations that can help you.

Substance use is not the solution. Substances may seem like they provide a temporary escape from your problems, but they are not the solution. Your problems will still be there when the substance wears off. To break the cycle of addiction, you need to find a healthy way to deal with the problems that are fueling your disease.

Don't give up. No matter your age or the severity of your addiction, it is never too late to ask for help in turning your life around. Start now.

Numerous resources are available to help teens overcome addiction. Many people your age are struggling with the same challenges. Now is always the best time to get help and change your life in a meaningful way. Addiction is a complicated disease with few easy fixes or simple answers. Educate yourself, ask for help when you need it, surround yourself with supportive friends and family, and you will be able to overcome this challenge.

—Joseph W. Ditre, PhD, Clinical Psychologist and Assistant Professor of Psychology, Texas A&M University, College Station, TX

WHAT IS ADDICTION? SYMPTOMS AND DEFINITIONS

Matt has a final tomorrow in biology, a class he needs to master if he wants to get into a good college. His stomach knots with stress. He can't focus on his textbook. To calm his nerves, he goes online and then texts his friends.

Many teens turn to drugs to cope with family problems or other issues. However, substance use can create a whole new set of problems.

At 10:15 p.m., Matt's just returned to studying when the front door slams. It's his dad, coming home drunk again. Matt's mom starts yelling. His dad screams. Matt cranks up the volume on his iPod, but he can still hear his parents' argument. Are they headed for another breakup? The knot in Matt's stomach tightens. He can't take this noise—his head is pounding. There's no way he'll get any more studying done tonight.

Tossing his textbook on the floor, Matt rummages in the back of his closet for the bottle. He sits on his bed, ready to stash it under his pillow. But the chances of his mom or dad barging in are slim. They hardly seem to notice him lately.

Matt gazes at the clear liquid, remembering his first drink at Kalil's birthday party a month ago. It didn't take much convincing from Kalil and the other guys for Matt to down a few beers and then a few more. He was curious, and everybody was having such a good time. The beer tasted great and totally loosened him up. Later, Matt swiped a bottle of vodka from his parents' bar. Now he can drink whenever he's stressed.

The first sip burns his throat. After a few more gulps, the knot in his stomach loosens, and he closes his eyes. He won't live at home forever, right? In two years he'll be off to college, away from his parents. He'll talk to Mr. Barlow in the morning about a makeup test. Matt smiles and takes another drink. Nothing matters except this beautiful floating feeling.

GETTING HOOKED

Like many people, Matt decided to start drinking because he was curious. He wanted to do the same cool stuff his friends were doing. The alcohol helped Matt loosen up. It made him feel good.

Now Matt has decided that drinking is a way to "take the edge off" his stress. It looks like he's drinking regularly. Is Matt on the way to becoming an alcoholic? It's hard to say. Is he *planning* on becoming an alcoholic? Of course not. No one wants to become addicted. So how does it happen? And why?

When you first take any psychoactive drug, you get a rush of pleasure—euphoria, self-confidence, power, relaxation, or satisfaction—depending on what substance you take. Drugs make you feel good because they stimulate a pleasure pathway in the brain, the same pathway triggered by activities such as eating delicious food and jumping into a

The younger you are when you start drinking, the more likely you are to become addicted.

swimming pool on a hot day. The motivation to seek pleasure is essential for survival—if people didn't enjoy eating, humans wouldn't last long.

ADDICTION AND THE BRAIN

When you experience something enjoyable, a chemical called dopamine floods the brain, causing you to feel happy or relaxed. After a period of time, the dopamine levels drop again. But unlike the gradual rise and fall of dopamine

TEEN ADDICTION

The problem of addiction is pretty big among teens. In 2009, 7 percent of US adolescents aged 12 to 17 abused or were dependent on substances (6.7 percent of boys and 7.4 percent of girls).[1]

levels from normal activities, addictive substances cause up to ten times the spike in your dopamine levels. The feeling of pleasure lasts longer and is more intense.

Whenever a behavior activates the pleasure pathway, the brain's desire for that behavior increases. As a result, you feel compelled to repeat the behavior. For example, after Matt had fun drinking beer at Kalil's party, his brain told him to look forward to drinking again. It began connecting drinking with pleasure.

If Matt starts getting drunk all the time, his brain will begin to bring its dopamine levels back to normal by lowering dopamine production. This means his high won't go as high or last as long, and his low will be deeper and last longer. Matt will develop a tolerance for alcohol, which means he will need to drink more—and more often—to get the same happy, floating feeling he had when he first started drinking.

If he continues drinking, Matt's pleasure pathway will completely derail and he'll crave alcohol just to feel normal. At this point, Matt will no longer be controlling the use of the substance; the substance will be controlling him. This is the definition of addiction. Even if addiction totally messes up his life and he wants to quit, the intense cravings will make stopping really tough.

SYMPTOMS AND DIAGNOSIS OF ADDICTION: USE, ABUSE, AND DEPENDENCE

Addiction doesn't start after just one drink, one pill, or one puff of a cigarette. It's a gradual process that moves from occasional use to wanting the substance all the time. Doctors and addiction specialists look for common symptoms, such as the following ones described in the American Psychiatric Association's *Diagnostic and Statistical Manual of Mental Disorders* (*DSM-IV*), to decide whether you're addicted to a substance and the severity of your addiction.[2]

Use. You sometimes drink alcohol or use drugs; you're able to stop when you want to and haven't had any problems related to drinking or taking drugs.

Abuse. Over a 12-month period of using drugs or alcohol, you experience one or more of the following:

- Not meeting your obligations, such as missing classes or not showing up for a job.

- Reckless behavior, such as driving while drunk.

- Having problems with school authorities or the law. This might include confrontations with teachers, being suspended or expelled from school, or being arrested.

- Using the substance even when it causes personal problems, such as major conflicts with your parents or breakups with a boyfriend or girlfriend.

Dependence. Dependence is basically the same thing as addiction, but in this case it refers to the next—and most serious—level of substance use. You would be diagnosed as dependent on a substance if you showed three or more of the following physical or behavioral symptoms over a 12-month period:

Physical

- Tolerance, which means you need more and more of the substance to get high.

- Withdrawal, which means you have physical or mental symptoms after you stop using, such as nausea or anxiety.

WHEN YOU START MAKES A DIFFERENCE

There's a strong relationship between drinking at an early age and eventual addiction. One study found that kids who began using alcohol at age 14 or younger were six times more likely to become addicted than young adults who started drinking at age 21.[3] Another study showed that of all adults addicted to alcohol, 95 percent started drinking before they were 21.[4]

If you are abusing a substance, you may be able to quit on your own. If you are dependent on a substance, reach out for help.

Behavioral

- As long as you have access to the substance, you're unable to stop using.

- You use more than you promised yourself you would.

- You spend more time using than participating in other activities.

- You spend lots of time obtaining or using the substance.

- Even if it's messing up your health, you continue using.

By the time you're dependent on a substance, it becomes more difficult to stop on your own. The good news is that with the right treatment, you can manage your addiction and work toward a life free of drugs.

SUBSTANCES MOST OFTEN USED BY TEENS

The Substance Abuse and Mental Health Services Administration (SAMHSA) reported in its *2009 National Survey on Drug Use and Health* the following rates for drug and alcohol use among American adolescents aged 12 to 17:

- Alcohol: 14.7 percent
- Tobacco: 11.6 percent (8.9 percent cigarettes, 2.3 percent smokeless tobacco).
- Illicit (Illegal) Drugs: 10 percent
    - Marijuana: 7.3 percent
    - Psychotherapeutics (nonmedical uses of prescription-type drugs): 3.1 percent
    - Inhalants: 1.0 percent
    - Hallucinogens: 0.9 percent
    - Ecstasy: 0.5 percent
    - Cocaine: 0.3 percent[5]

ASK YOURSELF THIS

- *Have you been to parties where alcohol, marijuana, or other drugs were easily available? What did you do and why? If you haven't yet been in that situation, what would you do and why?*

- *In what ways can you imagine Matt's life changing if he continues using alcohol?*

- *Like Matt, you have probably wanted to "take the edge off" your stress sometimes. What healthy things do you do to improve your mood?*

- *Do you have a friend you think may be addicted to a substance? What about his or her behavior makes you think so?*

- *Do you believe this friend's behavior is harmful to himself or herself and to others? In what ways?*

SMOKING CIGARETTES

While cigarette smoking has declined among teens in recent years, tobacco is still the second most commonly used drug after alcohol. Forty-six percent of high school students have tried smoking cigarettes, and every day in the United States approximately 4,000 adolescents between 12 and 17 try their first cigarette.[6]

IT'S NOT JUST ABOUT WILLPOWER: CAUSES AND RISK FACTORS

T anya sits next to her open bedroom window and takes her first hit of the day. The smoke billows into the frosty morning air along with her loneliness. For three years now, since she was 13 and her little brother

Being addicted to a substance doesn't mean you're weak. It means your genes and social environment make you more vulnerable to addiction.

died, Tanya has started her day with weed. It's relaxing. It keeps her depression away.

She coughs, a painful rasping from deep inside her chest. It's probably from the weed, but Tanya doesn't care. It's a small price to pay for feeling good. Hearing her mom in the hallway, Tanya stubs out her joint and shuts the window. Her mom is such a hypocrite—she orders Tanya not to use drugs, yet she uses them herself.

School is boring and a waste of time, but her friends are there, so that's where Tanya heads. First period slowly drags by. She tries to focus on Mrs. Cho's poetry lecture, but it's hard to concentrate. It's weird; she used to get good grades, especially in English. Now, as soon as she learns something, she seems to forget it.

At lunch, Tanya and her friends go off campus and smoke more bud. Allie offers the group free cocaine. When it comes to drugs, Tanya knows nothing is free—it's just a dealer's way of getting them hooked. But everyone else does it and Tanya shrugs, knowing she won't get addicted from snorting just one line.

Tanya tried to quit weed once, after she'd pinched bills from her mom's purse and gotten in big trouble. Plus, her dream of becoming a nurse was slipping away with every failed class. But right after stopping, her depression roared back and she couldn't sleep. She felt anxious, even suicidal. All she could think about was smoking. She finally gave in and started smoking again, figuring she was weak, one of those people who didn't have enough willpower to quit.

YOUR BRAIN, HIJACKED

In the past, almost everyone believed that when a person became addicted to drinking or taking drugs, it was a sign of weakness. Or they simply wanted to be addicted and it was a lifestyle choice.

The belief that addiction is a personal failing is still around. One poll found that while 76 percent of respondents thought addiction was a disease, this same group believed the biggest problem facing addicts was a "lack of willpower."[1] Scientific research is showing us that addiction is much more complicated than most people think. It's not just about willpower.

PEERING INSIDE THE BRAIN

Due to the development of brain-imaging scanning equipment such as computed tomography (CT), magnetic resonance imaging (MRI), and positron emission tomography (PET), the past few years have seen many advances in scientists' ability to look inside the living brain. Used while the patient is awake, these machines can show which chemicals, in addition to dopamine, are affected by alcohol and specific drugs. This research supports the idea that addiction changes the way the brain functions.

Your parents and friends may not understand why you can't just quit using. Addiction is a disease, so ask a trusted adult for help in getting treatment.

You've already learned that the pleasure pathway in your brain tells you to repeat things that feel good. But the brain also has a regulating system that is located in the prefrontal cortex, a part of the brain behind the forehead. The prefrontal cortex weighs options and potential consequences so you can make good decisions. It makes sure that what you're about to do is safe and in your—and everyone else's—best interests.

In a normally functioning brain, the pleasure and regulating systems are closely connected.

For example, your pleasure system would tell you to eat the last cookie on the plate at a party. But your regulating system reminds you that you've already eaten several cookies, that too many cookies are bad for your health, and that someone else might like to eat the last one.

In an addicted brain, the pleasure and regulating systems become disconnected, making it harder to think critically. Over time, this means addiction weakens your ability to make good decisions, while at the same time strengthening your desire to take the drug. It's as if the substance hijacks your brain, and getting and using the drug become your brain's main objective. Not only would your addicted brain compel you to eat that last cookie, but it would also make sure you searched for and ate even more cookies.

Unlike other brain diseases, the first step into addiction is voluntary—it is your decision to drink or take a drug. But once you have it, addiction is similar to many other brain diseases, such as schizophrenia, Parkinson's disease, Alzheimer's disease, and clinical depression.

RISK FACTORS FOR ADDICTION

Maybe someone you know uses the same substance you do, but she uses much less and seems able to stop whenever she wants.

The reasons one person moves from substance use to abuse and another person doesn't are complicated. Heredity, or your genes, and your social environment are big risk factors. Mental health issues, your age, the strength of the drug, and how it's taken also play roles in addiction.

Genes determine more than your height, eye color, and hair color. You can also inherit an increased risk for chronic diseases, such as diabetes, high blood pressure, and addiction. If your parents, siblings, or grandparents have an addiction, you're at greater risk of developing one. In fact, studies have shown that genes account for approximately 50 to 60 percent of all cases of addiction.[2]

If you never take drugs or drink alcohol, you'll never become addicted, regardless of your genetic makeup. So what causes people to start

MY PARENTS AREN'T ADDICTED, SO I'M NOT AT RISK, RIGHT?

Wrong. Just because your parents or other family members don't drink or use drugs doesn't mean you're not at risk for addiction. Many people without a genetic background of addiction still become addicted.

On the other hand, having an immediate family member with an addiction doesn't guarantee that you *will* become addicted. But it does mean you're at greater risk. Family history studies have shown that having one alcoholic parent increases your chances of becoming an alcoholic by one-third. Your chances are quadrupled if both parents are alcoholics, and the risk is nine times greater if both parents and a grandparent are alcoholics.[3]

High school can mean high pressure from friends to do drugs. Teens are at the highest risk of using on prom night and after graduation.

using in the first place? Your social environment is a significant factor.

Number one on the list of environmental influences is peer pressure. You may remember that Matt's buddies encouraged him to drink beer. And Tanya decided to snort cocaine after her friends used it. You're more likely to experiment with drugs and alcohol if that's what your friends are doing.

Your parents are also big influences on your behavior. They're your first role models, which means if your parents don't drink or use drugs, you probably won't see it as a good lifestyle choice either. The more closely your parents monitor you, and the more they are involved in your life, the less likely you'll be to use or abuse substances.

Stressful events in your life, such as physical, emotional, or sexual abuse, and physical trauma from illness, injury, natural disasters, or other accidents, can make it more likely that you'll use drugs or alcohol.

Another environmental factor is how easy or hard it is to score a substance. A person living in an isolated rural community, for example, will probably have less access to heroin and

ADDICTION AND THE MEDIA

Television, movies, and magazines portray drinking alcohol and taking drugs as fun, glamorous—even cool. But does what you see in the media really affect how you behave?

In one study, students stated that they were three times more likely to try alcohol after viewing multiple movie scenes showing adults drinking alcohol. Kids aged ten to 14 were more than twice as likely to start smoking after seeing smoking on-screen.[4]

Lawsuits against the tobacco industry in the 1990s revealed that tobacco companies targeted kids and teens in their advertising. Although tobacco companies are now restricted from intentionally marketing to children, advertisements for cigarettes and smokeless tobacco continue to be placed close to schools and playgrounds, and tobacco product ads are still published in magazines popular with teens.[5]

DRUG AVAILABILITY

According to the SAMHSA
2009 National Survey on Drug Use and Health,

Almost half (49.9 percent) of youths aged 12 to 17 reported in 2009 that it would be fairly easy or very easy for them to obtain marijuana if they wanted some. Approximately one in five reported it would be easy to get cocaine (20.9 percent). About one in seven (13.5 percent) indicated that LSD would be fairly or very easily available, and 12.9 percent reported easy availability for heroin.[7]

cocaine than a person in an urban setting. A societal acceptance of alcohol and drugs increases the likelihood of use.

AGE AND ADOLESCENT BRAIN DEVELOPMENT

The younger you are when you start drinking or using drugs, the more likely you are to become addicted. Recent scientific research shows that the adolescent brain is more susceptible to addiction than the adult brain. The prefrontal cortex does not fully mature until the age of 24 or 25, but the brain's pleasure pathways *are* fully developed by adolescence. The result is pleasure seeking without regulation, and a higher likelihood that teens will experiment with drugs and alcohol without thinking about the long-term consequences.[6] If you're already abusing drugs or alcohol, your ability to make healthy decisions is weakened even more by the negative effects addiction has on critical thinking skills.

Brains that aren't fully developed can change more easily, though. This means that teenage brains are better at repairing damage from drug use than adult brains, which don't change as easily.

MENTAL HEALTH ISSUES

Research shows that more than half of the young people who've been diagnosed with substance abuse also have a mental illness.[8] This is known as having co-occurring disorders, or a comorbidity. For the greatest chance of recovery from addiction, both disorders need to be treated.

MENTAL HEALTH DISORDERS LINKED TO ADDICTION

Drug and alcohol abuse have been linked to mental health disorders such as depression, bipolar disease, panic disorder, disruptive behavior (including conduct disorder), hyperactivity (including attention deficit hyperactivity disorder), and stress disorders (including post-traumatic stress disorder). The disorder itself can make you susceptible to dangerous behavior, such as drug abuse. And using substances can become a way to self-medicate as you try to deal with the discomfort and confusion of the disorder. Not only can mental health issues increase your risk of developing an addiction, but substance use can also trigger mental health disorders or make existing disorders worse.

Mental illness often fuels addiction, but being dependent on a substance can also make you more likely to develop a mental illness.

Even if you don't have a diagnosable mental illness, you may be struggling with psychological symptoms such as anxiety, loneliness, anger, sadness, or boredom. Tanya, for example, smoked marijuana partly to cope with her loneliness and depression.

METHOD OF ADMINISTRATION

Some drugs are more powerful than others and can quickly lead to addiction. Heroin and cocaine, for example, reach your brain faster and flood your brain with more dopamine than other drugs. How a drug is taken also affects addiction—the faster the body processes the substance and gets it to the brain, the greater the dopamine surge and chance of addiction. A drug that you drink or swallow reaches the brain the slowest. Snorting gets a drug into your system faster, and injection is faster still. Inhaling gets a drug to your brain the fastest.

ASK YOURSELF THIS

- *What evidence do you see that Tanya's decision-making skills have been hijacked by her addiction?*

- *Name four of Tanya's risk factors for addiction.*

- *Do you think it is likely or unlikely that Tanya will become addicted to cocaine? Why?*

- *Name three things you've done because you wanted to do what everyone else was doing. Would you have made the same choices if you'd been by yourself?*

- *Do you think your parents are good role models for not drinking or using drugs? Why or why not?*

SOBERING FACTS: COMPLICATIONS OF ADDICTION

A shwin is confused; he's totally out of it. Why is his face pressed against the pavement? He hears sirens. A searing pain shoots up his leg and through his arm. An accident. He was in a car accident! The impact

Never drive while intoxicated, and never ride with someone you know has been using. If you do, you are putting your life and the lives of others at risk.

must have thrown him out of Noah's Camaro. *But where's Noah? Is he okay?*

Ashwin tries to get up to check on his best friend, but his head swirls and someone gently pushes him down. "You're injured," a paramedic says. "Don't move."

"Noah . . ." Ashwin whispers hoarsely. He's having trouble talking. He's still wasted, his mind's a blur. What happened? He tries to piece it together.

They'd gone to a party after winning the basketball tournament. Ashwin remembers taking shots of tequila and chugging beer from a keg. Somebody was handing out pills. Ecstasy, he thinks. At that point, he didn't care what he was taking as long as it kept his buzz going. Plus, Tiffany was hanging all over him, and he liked his chances of scoring.

Then Noah had started feeling sick and said he needed to go home. Ashwin didn't want to leave, but Noah was his ride. He was also Ashwin's friend.

The paramedic checks his leg. Ashwin can't believe he didn't take Noah's keys and call someone for a ride—he could've called his sister or his dad. He didn't even fasten his stupid seat belt! The last thing he remembers is Noah

DRIVING UNDER THE INFLUENCE OF MARIJUANA

DUI-related vehicle accidents aren't just a result of too much alcohol. Accidents are also common with marijuana intoxication. A typical "recreational use" of marijuana is roughly equivalent to a .07 to .10 percent blood alcohol content, which in most states is enough for a DUI conviction.[2]

slumping over the steering wheel and the car swerving off the road.

Two paramedics are working on Ashwin now. The pain makes him wince, and he wonders how badly he's injured. He has a basketball scholarship to college next year. What if he's too messed up to play? As the paramedics turn him carefully onto his back, he catches a glimpse of Noah's beloved red Camaro. It's unrecognizable, the driver's side crumpled against a light post. Ashwin squeezes his eyes shut and pushes back tears. Noah's still in there. And there's no way he's alive.

INJURIES AND ACCIDENTS

Chances are, you know someone like Ashwin or Noah who's been injured or killed in a car crash. Among Americans aged ten to 24, almost one-third (32.3 percent) of all fatalities are from motor vehicle accidents.[1]

Alcohol and drugs are often linked to vehicle crashes, making death and injury from accidents one of the most tragic complications of using drugs and alcohol. In 2004, 20 percent of twelfth graders drove after drinking alcohol. Thirty percent of all students rode at least once during the prior 30 days of the study with a driver who'd been drinking alcohol.[3] Each year, it's estimated that 5,000 people under age 21 die in accidents—car crashes, homicides, suicides, falls, fires, and drownings—all as a result of underage drinking.[4] And you're mistaken if you think only alcohol causes accidents. All drugs affect motor skills, judgment, and reaction time.

HEALTH PROBLEMS

If you're an adolescent abusing alcohol or drugs, you're facing many potential complications. Taking drugs in high doses or mixing them with other drugs can result in overdose, which can lead to unconsciousness, coma, and death.

While you might not develop full-fledged liver

MARIJUANA AND TRIPS TO THE ER

Marijuana is the primary cause of emergency room visits for adolescents. Delusions, hallucinations, vehicle accidents, and negative reactions from combinations with other drugs are the main complaints. For adults, the leading cause of emergency room visits is alcohol.[5]

disease, heavy alcohol usage can increase liver enzymes, which is a sign of liver damage. Heavy adolescent drinking can hinder the normal development of reproductive organs in both boys and girls, and using steroids can cause changes in sex hormones. Marijuana, cocaine, methamphetamine, and heroin can damage the immune system, and alcohol has been shown to stunt bone growth in boys.

In addition to the long-term effects of smoking cigarettes, such as heart disease, stroke, chronic lung disease, and various cancers, smoking by young people can lead to immediate respiratory problems. Using smokeless tobacco can also increase the risks of heart disease and stroke and can lead to cancers of the mouth and throat. Drug abusers who use needles are more likely to contract infectious diseases, such as HIV, from sharing needles. Alcohol and drug use are linked with mental

ALCOHOL AND ENERGY DRINKS

While there may be little risk associated with downing an energy drink now and then, a 2009 study showed that combining alcohol with the high levels of caffeine in energy drinks can leave you feeling "wide awake and drunk." This can mask how impaired you are and lead to unsafe behavior. This same study also found a connection between frequently consuming energy drinks and developing alcohol dependence.[6]

Someone who has overdosed may appear to be sleeping and fail to respond to sound or touch. If you think someone has overdosed, call 911.

health problems, such as depression and anxiety disorder.

OTHER COMPLICATIONS

If you use alcohol or drugs, you're more likely to have unprotected sex with more partners, increasing your risk of contracting sexually transmitted diseases, including HIV. You're also more likely to be a rape victim than a teen who does not drink or use drugs. Adolescents who drink or use drugs are more likely to commit suicide.

Using drugs or alcohol can increase conflict with family and friends and problems at school, including low motivation and poor grades. It may be difficult to hold down a job due to absences and poor work performance. You may be arrested and end up with legal problems if you steal to support your habit, receive a DUI, get into fights, or sell drugs. Addictive substances aren't cheap, and it's easy to end up with financial problems as you try to support your habit.

In addition to these more general complications, every substance has short- and long-term physical and emotional effects. For example, amphetamines can cause short-term irregular heartbeat, irritability, paranoia, and insomnia, along with long-term high blood pressure and

VOMITING

Puking may be gross, but it's your body's defense mechanism for getting rid of poisons. If you pass out from consuming too much alcohol too quickly, the part of the brain that controls vomiting can stop working. Without vomiting, dangerous amounts of alcohol can stay in your stomach, resulting in coma or death.

The most common diseases spread by sharing needles are HIV, hepatitis B, and hepatitis C.

mood changes. You can find more information on specific drugs and their effects in reference books at your school or public library, or on Web sites. Being informed about the consequences of drug and alcohol use may guide you to making better choices when you encounter addictive substances.

Substance addiction complicates nearly every aspect of your life, including relationships with the people you care about most.

ASK YOURSELF THIS

- *Have you ever driven or engaged in other risky behavior while intoxicated? What happened? How do you know when you're too intoxicated to act safely?*

- *Like Ashwin, have you ever felt like you should have prevented an intoxicated person from driving? How did you handle it, or how would you handle it if you haven't been in this situation before?*

HEAVY DRINKING IN TEENS

Teens who drink alcohol are at high risk for short- and long-term physical and emotional problems because adolescents who drink tend to drink a lot. Teens have an average of five drinks per session. By comparison, adults age 26 and older have an average of two to three drinks per session.[7]

- *Imagine Ashwin's life a year from now, then five years and ten years from now. What's he like? Do you think he'll ever get over Noah's death?*

- *Besides accidents, which complications mentioned in this chapter do you think are the most severe? Why?*

- *If you use marijuana, what symptoms of addiction do you have? In what ways has your behavior changed since you started smoking? (If you don't use marijuana, answer these questions thinking about someone you may know who uses it.)*

TREATMENT, PART I: GETTING HELP AND DETOX

Michael knows all about addiction. He studied it in his health and psychology classes, and they've had two assemblies at school on the dangers of drugs. The only thing all that information's done for him is given him more ideas for getting high.

Even when you're a teen, addiction has real consequences.

Yeah, maybe his grades aren't the best, and he doesn't give a crap about much of anything, but give up his bud? No way. That would be like giving up his best friend, and why would he do that? A 'j' will fix anything. When Kiara broke up with him last month, he got high. When he got a D on his chemistry midterm, he got high. It was cloudy this morning, so he got high. Now it's mid-morning, he's bored, and he'll toke again before his next class.

He's just lit up when he hears, "Michael. Put that out and come with me." Snap. It's Principal Lee, giving him a death stare.

Michael follows him to the office. The school has a no-drug policy and Michael has broken it for, what, the fifth time? When Principal Lee tells Michael, "This is it," Michael thinks he'll be suspended for two weeks instead of the usual one. But then he sees a cop car pull into the parking lot. Arrested? No effing way!

The cop handcuffs him and throws him into the squad car. He gets processed at juvie. He's never been arrested before and he's terrified. His high is wearing off, and he could really use a hit.

When he goes to court, Michael's parents are all for him getting treatment. So is the judge. She gives him a lecture about straightening out his life, blah, blah, blah. He wishes he could tell these losers he doesn't need treatment, but they won't listen.

THE FIRST STEPS

Research tells us it's only when the consequences of addiction become severe that people finally decide to change their behavior and get treatment. But adolescents don't often suffer severe consequences for their addictions. Like Michael, most teens end up in treatment not because they want to go, but because their parents, the courts, schools, or the social service system sends them there.

Maybe you recognize that you have a problem with drugs or alcohol and want to stop. Fights with your parents are getting worse, and your grades are sliding south. You think you're slipping from use into abuse.

FOUR REASONS TEENS DON'T SEEK TREATMENT

- **Health problems haven't fully taken effect. For example, it takes years for liver disease to develop.**
- **Not only do teens usually have a safety net of parents or other relatives, they have fewer big responsibilities— such as kids, a spouse, a job, or a mortgage—that will fall apart if their addiction gets out of control.**
- **Their immature prefrontal cortex makes teens less able to see that their addictive behavior is harmful.**
- **The pleasures of substance addiction initially seem to outweigh the negatives.**

Quitting on your own can be tough. Having friends and family who support your decision to get clean can make all the difference.

The fact is, most people stop using drugs and alcohol on their own. Here are a few self-help steps you can take:

- Make two lists, with the benefits of using on one side and the costs of using on the other. The costs of using will probably outweigh the benefits, and seeing this in writing can help you commit to stopping.

- Write down your short-term and long-term goals related to quitting. For example, "I will stop smoking marijuana on school

Addiction specialists are experts in your disease. They treat drug and alcohol addiction, eating disorders, gambling addiction, and other disorders.

days." Then write down how you're going to accomplish your goals.

- Follow the recommendations in Chapters 6 and 7 on avoiding triggers and enlisting your friends for help.

- If emotional issues are interfering with staying away from substances, talk to a trusted adult and learn how to begin counseling sessions.

WHEN QUITTING BY YOURSELF DOESN'T WORK

If you've tried to stop using by yourself and can't, or if you're at the point of substance dependence, it's time to consider getting professional treatment. Kicking addiction by yourself is really tough and doesn't work for most people. Remember that addiction is a disease of the brain; in the same way a person with epilepsy would see a medical professional

YOUR FIRST VISIT WITH AN ADDICTION SPECIALIST

Your first visit with a professional about your addiction may be at a doctor's office, in a hospital, or at a treatment center. People qualified to diagnose addiction can include medical doctors (pediatricians, general practitioners, psychiatrists) and psychologists. Or you might see a psychiatric nurse, mental-health counselor, clinical social worker, or treatment intake specialist. If the professional you first see is not qualified to diagnose addiction, ask to be referred to someone who is qualified.

The addiction specialist will ask you a lot of questions about your drinking or drug-using habits and about your family and lifestyle. This person will then compare your answers to the symptoms of abuse and dependence in order to decide where you are on the addiction spectrum and what kind of treatment will work best for you.

It's important to be honest when answering these questions. Don't be embarrassed. The clinician will respect you as an individual, and your story is nothing he or she hasn't heard before. And make sure to ask questions if you have them.

for help, it makes just as much sense to see an expert for help with addiction.

A good first step is finding someone you can trust and talk to. A friend can fill this role. Then find a supportive adult to tell. This adult might be a parent or other relative, teacher, school counselor, school nurse, doctor, or religious leader. An adult can look at all your options and take the next steps for finding you help, such as a treatment program. Treatment generally passes though three phases of care: detoxification (detox), rehabilitation (rehab), and continuing aftercare.

TREATMENT BY THE NUMBERS

- The number of people aged 12 or older who reported receiving treatment for the following substances in the US in 2009 were:
    - Alcohol: 2.9 million
    - Marijuana: 1.2 million
    - Cocaine: 787,000
    - Pain relievers: 739,000
    - Stimulants: 517,000
    - Heroin: 507,000
    - Hallucinogens: 443,000
    - Tranquilizers: 421,000[1]
- Less than 10 percent of American adolescents aged 12 to 17 get the treatment they need for drug or alcohol problems.[2]
- Marijuana is the drug of choice for most adolescents starting a treatment program.[3]

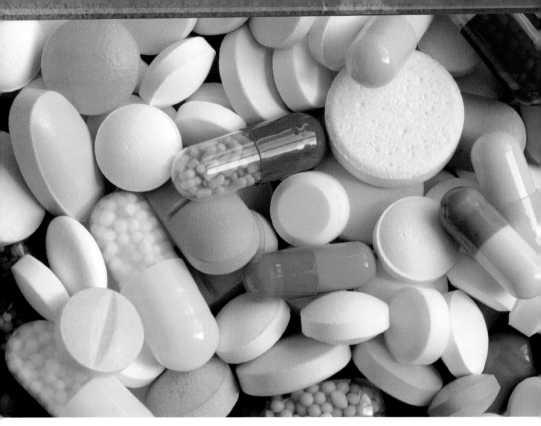

Medications can be used during withdrawal to ease symptoms or during treatment to suppress cravings, but these medications can also be addictive.

TREATMENT FOR WITHDRAWAL: DETOX

The first goal of treatment is to get the addictive substance out of your body. Depending on your level of dependence and the substance you're using, the first step in treatment may be a few days spent at a hospital or inpatient facility. This will allow you to rid your body of the addictive substance through a process called detoxification. Detox is best done under medical supervision, and you might be given medication to lessen your withdrawal symptoms.

WITHDRAWAL SYMPTOMS

Category of Drug	Substances	Withdrawal Symptoms
Depressants[4]	Alcohol, barbiturates, benzodiazepines (including Valium, Xanax, Ativan, Klonopin, sleeping pills)	Insomnia, anxiety, depression, seizures, hallucinations, delirium
Stimulants[5]	Cocaine, crack cocaine, methamphetamine, amphetamine (including Adderall and Dexedrine), and Ritalin	Depression, fatigue, anxiety, intense cravings, suicidal thoughts, paranoia, psychosis
Opiates[6]	Heroin, morphine, prescription painkillers (including codeine, OxyContin, Percocet, Vicodin)	Sleeplessness, depression, rapid pulse, rapid breathing, high blood pressure, abdominal cramps, tremors, bone and muscle pain, vomiting, diarrhea
Hallucinogens[7]	LSD, MDMA (Ecstasy), Ketamine hydrochloride, PCP	Only MDMA is considered to have withdrawal symptoms: fatigue, anxiety, loss of appetite, difficulty concentrating, depression
Cannabis[8]	Marijuana	Cravings, irritability, insomnia, anxiety
Nicotine[9]	Cigarettes, chewing tobacco	Cravings, headache, anxiety, nausea, irritability, depression, fatigue

Once your body is "clean" and is no longer under the influence of drugs or alcohol, the task of rehabilitation—of learning to live without an addictive substance—begins.

ASK YOURSELF THIS

- *What is your school's policy on drugs and alcohol? What would you change about it if you could?*

- *If you've been in treatment for addiction before, was it your idea or someone else's? Did you think you needed help then, or that you need help now?*

- *Which adults in your life do you trust to get you help with addiction treatment? Think of at least two.*

- *What would you say to these supportive adults if and when you need help with addiction?*

- *What kinds of questions might you ask a doctor or other clinician about addiction?*

TREATMENT, PART II:
REHAB

Shannon hated her mom for sending her
to drug treatment. At first she thought
Lake Vista Rehab was a total joke, from
the strict and nosy staff to the pathetic addicts
she was forced to live with 24–7. Then in a
peer group session, it turned out that everyone

A good rehab program will help you learn how to face your problems and meet your goals without using substances.

thought the same thing about her. Now Shannon realizes she's not so different from the other addicts, and maybe rehab isn't such a bad idea after all.

She misses the numb, warm feeling she got from OxyContin. Shannon still craves the drug, especially while lounging in her room during free time when unwelcome thoughts creep in. Facing life sober can pretty much suck.

But being sober definitely has its good points. She doesn't miss being strung out and stressing over getting pills—first stealing from her mom's medicine cabinet and then buying over the Internet. It was pretty nerve-racking, not to mention expensive. And she's starting to remember what it was like to have goals.

Lake Vista is full of farm animals, and when the residents aren't in school, meetings, or counseling sessions, they're assigned to take care of the chickens, pigs, and goats. At first the farm chores grossed her out, but the squeaky little piglets were cute, and now she's really into it. She's decided she'd like to be a veterinarian.

When Shannon was high, all she thought about was scoring her next pill. Knowing she has a goal for her future that she can actually reach is its own rush. Shannon's release date is a month away. It seems like forever and no time at all. She's excited about going home, but she's also scared. Will she be able to deal with problems that come up without using Oxy? Or will she go back to the same old thing? She's motivated and has things she wants to accomplish, but it's all a big fat question mark in her head. She doesn't know what's going to happen.

ARE YOU READY FOR REHAB?

Whether you choose to seek addiction rehabilitation treatment on your own, or if, like Shannon, it's been chosen for you, the good news is that it can be just as effective either way. And the sooner you get treatment, the greater your chance of success. The popular myth that you have to hit rock bottom for treatment to work just isn't true.

PRESCRIPTION DRUG ABUSE

Shannon's drug of choice, OxyContin, is a legally prescribed pain reliever. The abuse of "Oxy" and other prescription medications such as Ritalin, Dexadrine, Valium, Vicodin, and Xanax, has tripled among teens since the 1990s.[1] Why the increase? Doctors prescribe more of these drugs every year, which means that teens have easier access to the drugs from friends or the family medicine cabinet. The drugs are also readily available on the Internet. The glut of pharmaceutical ads in magazines and on television can make using prescription drugs seem safe, which they are if taken as directed to treat a serious health problem, but there's a big risk for addiction and overdose.

There are many rehab options, and it's important to choose a program that's a good fit for you. The best programs for teens are the ones designed just for adolescents. As we've already explored, adolescent addiction differs from adult addiction in many ways—the chances are pretty good your problems, stresses, and goals aren't the same as those of an adult with a full-time job and kids.

The two general categories of rehab treatment programs are inpatient and outpatient. In an inpatient program, you live full-time at a special facility or in a hospital. Inpatient programs are also called residential programs. In an outpatient program, you live at home and go to treatment part-time.

While statistics show that most adolescents end up in a two-hour-a-week outpatient program, the type of rehab program you enter will depend on a few factors.[2]

Cost. Long-term inpatient programs for teens are effective, but they're also the most expensive and might not be completely covered by insurance.

Programs in your area. If you need to stay close to home for treatment, you'll be limited to the programs near you. This might mean going to an outpatient support group that includes adults.

Court requirements. If you're legally required to attend substance-abuse treatment, there may be a rehab program the court expects you to attend for a certain amount of time.

If you've been to treatment before. Most kids end up going to treatment two to four times before they're able to stay sober.[3] If you've tried outpatient programs and you're still relapsing, it may be time for a residential program.

Home environment. A supportive family can make an outpatient program a good choice. But if people at home are using drugs or alcohol, or if it's really tough for you to stay away from friends who use, residential treatment might be the best choice.

Mental health issues. As previously mentioned, more than half of the teens who have a substance addiction also have a mental health disorder, such as anxiety, depression,

OTHER REHAB OPTIONS

Private Therapy. **If being in a group program doesn't seem right for you, consider getting individual counseling from a therapist experienced in addiction treatment. A private therapist is also a good option if your treatment program doesn't include care for any mental health issues you may have, such as anxiety or depression.**

Clergy. **Seeing a religious leader trained in addiction treatment can be a good choice if you prefer a religious path to sobriety.**

Twelve-Step Programs. **These are free self-help groups, such as Alcoholics Anonymous (AA) and Narcotics Anonymous (NA).**

Many states offer programs to help juvenile offenders turn their lives around and even earn their GEDs.

panic disorder, attention deficit disorder, conduct disorder, trauma, and others.[4] If you have co-occurring disorders, it's important to treat both issues for the best chance of success with your addiction recovery. This may mean going to an inpatient or outpatient program with a full range of mental health services, or seeing a therapist while also attending an addiction support group.

WHAT HAPPENS IN A TEEN REHAB PROGRAM?

The main goal of both inpatient and outpatient teen rehab programs is to change your behavior so you can live drug-free. This can include learning about addiction, exploring new ways to cope with daily stress, and figuring out how to avoid old places, activities, and people that might cause you to use again.

You might also work on emotional and mental health problems. Some programs may include urine drug testing to make sure you're

CAN I STOP MY ADDICTION WITH A PILL?

Not really. First, only alcohol and opiates (heroin and painkillers) have prescription medications that are shown to help with addiction withdrawal and treatment, and even then addiction medications need to be combined with therapy for best results. Plus, medications aren't often prescribed to anyone under 18.

If your doctor decides medication is a good choice, you might be prescribed one of the following drugs for alcohol dependence. Naltrexone decreases cravings by reducing the "high" from drinking. Disulfiram creates a negative physical reaction from drinking. Acamprosate normalizes derailed brain activity. Topiramate is a promising drug currently in clinical trials; it's an antiepileptic medication that is shown to reduce alcohol cravings.

For opiate addiction, Methadone helps prevent withdrawal symptoms and cravings, but it is also an addictive substance. Buprenophine works in a similar way to Methadone but with less chance of addiction or overdose. Naltrexone prevents an opiate high but doesn't prevent cravings.

staying clean during treatment. Families, especially parents or guardians, are often involved in drug education, group sessions, counseling, and parenting classes to learn better discipline skills and how to support your recovery. Your experience will be different depending on whether you choose inpatient or outpatient treatment.

Inpatient. Inpatient or residential treatment, the type of program Shannon attended, involves living at a facility for a few months to a year with other adolescents going through the same treatment. Residential treatment is sometimes called "taking a time out," because it gives you time away from addictive substances and everything associated with your old lifestyle, including friends and places where you used to hang out.

These programs are usually highly structured and supervised, with scheduled therapy sessions (including individual, group, and family), drug education, support groups, and activities. You'll also take school classes so you don't fall behind in your education.

Outpatient. Outpatient rehab programs are similar to residential programs, including therapy sessions, drug education, support groups, life skills, and goal setting classes, but you only attend part-time. You might attend four or five afternoons and evenings a week in the beginning, then gradually go less often.

An advantage of outpatient treatment is that you don't have to leave your home or school, and you have support while you find drug-free friends and activities and work on family issues. Not leaving home is also a disadvantage, because you still have easy access to old friends and places where you used to drink or do drugs.

Rehab is a great start to your recovery, but it's not the end of treatment. Addiction is a chronic disease. To avoid relapse, it's best to continue your recovery efforts with some kind of aftercare.

RESIDENTIAL REHAB CHECKLIST

Besides interesting activities, clean facilities, and good food, high-quality residential treatment programs for teens have a few things in common:

- They are designed specifically for teens.
- They last three to 12 months.
- They involve families in the treatment process.
- They have an adequate staff of qualified professionals.
- They have accredited educational programs that won't let you fall behind in school.
- They have an upbeat and positive atmosphere.
- They have proven records of success based on the number of people finishing the program and graduates who are still drug-free.
- They provide an aftercare program.

ASK YOURSELF THIS

- *Why did Shannon see the others at Lake View Rehab as addicts, yet she didn't see herself that way?*

- *Do you believe you don't have to hit rock bottom for treatment to work? Why or why not?*

- *What about residential rehab would be hardest for you? How would you deal with the things you didn't like?*

- *What are some other advantages and disadvantages to outpatient treatment?*

- *Can you relate to Shannon's fear of going home after treatment? What advice would you give her?*

TOBACCO TREATMENT

The nicotine in cigarettes is very tough to quit. Studies have shown that nicotine is addictive in similar ways to heroin, cocaine, and alcohol, and young people face the same withdrawal symptoms as adults. One survey found that 51 percent of current high school smokers tried to quit during the 12 months before the survey was taken.[5] As with all forms of addiction, relapse is common and there isn't one treatment program that works best for everyone. A good first step is to ask an adult you trust for help.

AFTERCARE, TRIGGERS, AND RELAPSE: RECOVERY

Michael lowers the top on his dad's convertible and backs out of the garage. His parents are letting him drive the car as a reward for finishing his six-week treatment program. He's totally stoked the three-afternoon-a-week rehab is over—*what*

Being free from drugs and the strict routine of rehab can feel great. Participating in an aftercare program will help keep you free from addiction.

a time suck. He had the option of joining an aftercare support group but talked his parents out of it. He's getting back into running, and more treatment will just interfere with his training schedule.

He learned a lot in treatment, more than he thought he would. The group sessions were cool. He and the other kids shared a lot of stuff. They talked about the advantages of not being high all the time, such as getting better grades and having fewer fights with their parents. The random urine tests were a pain, but it was one of the things that kept Michael from using; he does not want to get arrested again.

The sun on Michael's arms feels great as he drives across town. He dips under the bridge near school and has a sudden overpowering urge to light up—the underpass is a place he smoked pot after school. He learned in treatment about cravings, and that it's important to stay away from triggers. The thing is, everything reminds him of getting high—stress, the scent of any kind of smoke, hearing the music he played when he got high.

Instead of the stoners he used to hang out with, Michael's been chilling with old friends from elementary school. They don't use and they're supportive, but even tagging along to

Twelve-step programs can be used as treatment or aftercare. These programs are effective and usually free.

the movies reminds him of getting stoned. He's supposed to meet those guys at the mall. But he parks the car in front of Kiara's house. She wants to hook up again. She's a party girl and Michael knows it's a big risk, but he's got the tools. He can handle it.

POST-REHAB: THE REAL DEAL

Does Michael have the tools to keep from getting high again? Unfortunately, most teens relapse during the first three months after treatment.[1] That's why being in some kind of aftercare for at least 90 days, and up to a year, is important. Some people stay in aftercare for the rest of their lives.

Aftercare services are designed to help keep you from relapsing. They do this by keeping tabs on your mental health, reminding you why you're choosing to stay sober, and supporting you while you change to a substance-free lifestyle, such as finding new friends and trying new activities. Aftercare services need to be close to where you live and not in an inpatient setting, since the point of aftercare is to support you in your normal life.

Aftercare can take many forms and may include one or a combination of the following services:

ALCOHOLICS ANONYMOUS

Alcoholics Anonymous (AA) was founded in 1935. The meetings are anonymous, free, and open to anyone. Run completely by volunteers, the one-hour meetings are held at all times of the day and night in locations across the United States. While there is a spiritual component to AA, it's not connected to any religion, and a spiritual belief isn't required.

Members talk openly about their struggles and successes with recovery, and they give each other nonjudgmental encouragement and support. Approximately 10 percent of AA members are under the age of 30, and they can attend any open meeting.[2] Some communities have programs just for young adults. You can get more information about AA, including meeting times and locations, at www.aa.org.

- Therapy groups or support groups, such as the once-a-week teen group Michael could have joined after his treatment program ended. Adolescent residential and outpatient rehab programs often include these groups as part of the services they provide.

- Twelve-step recovery groups, such as Alcoholics Anonymous (AA) and Narcotics Anonymous (NA), which are free self-help support groups.

- Individual sessions with a therapist, either as a continuation of your rehab treatment or as a separate aftercare service.

- Family therapy to work on issues you may have with your parents or guardians or siblings.

- Follow-up phone calls from a counselor in your rehab program.

OTHER 12-STEP PROGRAMS

Other self-help addiction organizations that use a 12-step approach include Narcotics Anonymous (for people addicted to drugs other than alcohol), Al-Anon and Alateen (for friends and family of alcoholics), Cocaine Anonymous, Crystal Meth Anonymous, Marijuana Anonymous, Gamblers Anonymous, Overeaters Anonymous, and many more. Some groups hold meetings online.

Twelve-step programs are effective aftercare. One study found that 46 percent of people participating in a 12-step program were still sober one year after finishing their rehab treatment program, compared to 36 percent of people who participated in behavioral therapy as their aftercare service.[3]

- Medication treatment, if appropriate and prescribed by a doctor, to help you manage substance cravings.

- Alternative therapies, including acupuncture, meditation, hypnosis, biofeedback, massage and bodywork, yoga, and religious-based programs.

To help you stay motivated and stick with your treatment plan, you might be required to submit urine tests. Positive motivations might include tokens or gifts when you reach certain recovery milestones.

As with rehab treatment, aftercare needs to be a good fit for you. And it's important to keep going. Your goal in recovery is to get to the point where you're confidently managing your cravings and creating a happy life without drugs or alcohol. So how do you manage cravings? For that answer, we first need to explore triggers and how they function.

TRIGGERS

Triggers are the sights, sounds, smells, feelings, thoughts, and activities that remind you of using drugs or alcohol. Michael's triggers included feeling stressed, seeing the underpass where he used to smoke marijuana, and hearing the music he played when he got high.

Addiction alters the functioning of the brain. In an addicted brain, the pleasure system is so out of control that your brain thinks it needs the addictive substance all the time in order to survive. The addicted brain enlists your senses and emotions to make sure you use the drug again. Your senses take only a fraction of a second to do their jobs and trigger a response from you, which you feel as an intense craving for the substance.

This process is so quick that the decision-making portion of your brain doesn't get a chance to weigh in. If it did, it might say, "Are you nuts? You just got arrested for doing this exact same thing last week and you're about to do it again? No way."

Rehab and aftercare help you manage cravings by identifying your triggers and teaching you ways to avoid them. Then the decision-making part of your brain has a fighting chance to be heard.

AFTERCARE ALTERNATIVES

Alternative therapies can be used as aftercare, either at the same time as other treatment programs or by themselves. Spiritual approaches use religious teachings to aid in addiction recovery. Acupuncture and massage focus on balancing the physical body. Meditation and biofeedback aim to help you relax your body and mind. Yoga combines a physical and a meditative approach. Art, dance, drama, music, and poetry are used to reduce stress, let you express your inner self, and raise your self-esteem. In sports-oriented therapy, the natural endorphins you get from exercise are used as an alternative to drugs.

Even if you've been successfully avoiding drugs or alcohol for months or years, something out-of-the-ordinary might happen: your parents split up, you go to a party after the prom and someone hands you a frosty beer, you don't get into the college you'd had your heart set on. You're vulnerable, the cravings win out, and you use again. You relapse.

FAMILY INVOLVEMENT

Studies show that treatment is most successful when at least one supportive family member is involved with your treatment.[4] Maybe your relationship with your parents is so tense there's no way you want them involved in your recovery process. Reach out to a sibling, uncle or aunt, cousin, or grandparent if you feel your parents will make the recovery process more difficult. The more involved your family is, the better they're going to understand what you're going through and how to best support you.

RELAPSE

Relapse does not mean failure. Think of it in relationship to other chronic diseases. If you were diabetic and ate too many cupcakes, would you feel so horrible about your mistake that you'd continue eating cupcakes? Probably not. You'd likely make adjustments to your insulin, cut back on your sugar intake, and quickly return to your treatment plan.

It needs to be the same with substance relapse: quickly return to your treatment plan,

Don't let a relapse send you into a downward spiral. Evaluate what triggered your relapse, and adjust your recovery plan to avoid those triggers in the future.

make whatever changes to treatment you think are necessary—such as going to your support group twice a week instead of once, or adding AA to your individual counseling—and try again. As with many chronic illnesses, relapse is a part of the disease of addiction. Most people go through treatment three or four times before they're successful.[5]

Avoiding relapse means dealing with triggers. That means changing your behavior. It also means changing your lifestyle.

ASK YOURSELF THIS

- *What incentives does Michael have for staying sober? Do you think they're enough to keep him from relapsing?*

- *What is Michael doing right to avoid triggers?*

- *What are your triggers? Name at least five.*

- *What red flags do you see in Michael's thoughts and behaviors that tell you he may be about to relapse? If he did relapse, what would you recommend he do next?*

- *Imagine one unusual situation that might spur you to relapse. How would you handle the situation to keep from using?*

EVALUATING TREATMENT AFTER RELAPSE

Relapse is a good time to figure out what is and isn't working with your recovery program. You can do this by asking yourself a few questions: What was I feeling and thinking when I relapsed? What triggers led to my craving? How will I avoid those triggers in the future? If I can't avoid the triggers, how will I handle them differently? What *is* working in my recovery program? What am I doing right? Knowing the answers to these tough questions will help you avoid a future relapse.

A SOBER LIFESTYLE: COPING WITH ADDICTION

Blake drags himself up the stairs and through the school doors. He's been sober for six months this time, but he still feels like he has to put on mental armor every time he steps onto campus.

Committing to a sober lifestyle means committing to friends and activities that support your recovery.

"What's up, man?" Carlos is leaning against the door.

"Not much," Blake says. He and Carlos have known each other for a few years, but they didn't really connect until they joined the same aftercare support group.

"You seem kinda down. Something going on with you?" Carlos asks.

Blake thinks about it. "Yeah. Got in a bad fight with the 'rents last night. I'm in a mind-obliterating mood."

Carlos winces. "Sorry, man. No worries. I've got your back."

They walk down the main hallway together in an arrangement they worked out—kind of their own mini-support group. They get to school just before the bell rings so there's not much time for socializing with old pals. They check in with each other, and if either of them is having a bad morning, they hang out as much as they can.

Halfway to their first period classes, Blake sees a deal go down—a subtle nod, hands barely touching as they exchange money for drugs. He recognizes the signals because for three years he was one of those guys buying and selling. The deals go on all day, every day. Kids get high all day, every day.

The bills in Blake's pocket feel as heavy as bricks. It would be so easy to blow his week's lunch money on something much more appetizing than cafeteria food.

Carlos must sense Blake's thoughts, because he nudges Blake's arm. "Take a deep breath, dude. Give me two reasons why you don't want to relapse."

Blake breathes and answers, "Med school. Elizabeth."

"Feel better?"

Blake nods. Going to college and keeping his girlfriend around are his biggest incentives for staying sober. And since his last relapse, he's been doing well. Really well. "I don't want to blow it this time," he says.

"I know, man. Neither do I."

COMMITTING TO CHANGE

Like Blake and Carlos, you can probably walk into school on any given day and have access to drugs or alcohol. If you were an adult, you might be able to pick up and move away from old friends and places that trigger using. But that's harder for teens to do.

Recovery means making a new identity for yourself—finding friends who don't use, activities that don't include mind-altering substances, and coping strategies to deal with problems without getting high.

Is changing your lifestyle tough? Definitely. But thousands of teens get sober every year, which means there's a lot to be hopeful for. The following are some suggestions to keep in mind as you continue on your path to addiction recovery.

DON'T USE

Don't use drugs or alcohol. Ever. Even a little. Research has shown that once you are dependent on a substance, attempts to cut back to moderate use often fail, resulting in relapse. By abstaining from drugs and alcohol, you are giving yourself the best chance to make a permanent recovery.

ADD STRUCTURE TO YOUR LIFE

So you've finished a structured rehab program where every moment of your day was filled with some group, class, or activity. Now you're home, you've got a lot of free time again, and you're filling the empty space with thoughts about getting high. A schedule can give you some of the control you had in rehab. Start by making a chart listing the hours of the day. Then fill every time block with an activity: eating, going to school, chores, homework, exercise, sleeping, attending a support group, or other positive activities. Follow your schedule. If you're still having trouble, give a copy of your schedule to a family member or someone else close to you. Ask them to help you stick with your new routine.

STAY IN AFTERCARE

One of the most important things you can do on your quest for a drug-free identity is to stay in an aftercare program. Not only is it a place to learn about and practice staying sober, but it can also be a great place to meet new friends who share your goals.

TAKE CARE OF YOURSELF

In the midst of an addiction, how you look and feel may not seem all that important. Not taking care of yourself can lead to a lack of self-esteem. Here are a few tips for developing a healthier lifestyle that will help you gain confidence:

Exercise. Not only does exercise make you feel and look better, but the endorphins produced by physical exertion can also give you a natural high.

Change your look. Get a haircut or style your hair differently. If you can afford it, change your wardrobe, or find new ways to mix and match the clothes you have. Now that you're sober, think about what look goes with the identity you've chosen for yourself.

Eat healthfully. Good nutrition is great fuel for a healthy mind. Eating healthfully might include cutting down on junk food, eating a few

Playing sports is a healthy way to have fun with friends, and exercise can produce a natural high.

more fruits and vegetables, or remembering to grab breakfast before school.

ACCEPT HELP

You need people in your life who respect your decision to stay sober. If they aren't 100 percent supportive, find people who are. Accept whatever help your friends and family offer. This might include calling someone up in the middle of the night when you're going through a rough time, or asking for a ride if you are in an unsafe situation.

FIND SAFE ACTIVITIES

Going to a party where you're pretty sure drugs or alcohol will be available is probably not the best idea—especially when you're in the early stages of recovery and feeling insecure about cravings and peer pressure. Even activities free from drugs and alcohol can trigger cravings if they happen in places where you used to get high. Remember what happened when Michael drove through the underpass?

HAVE A PLAN

Since triggers can cue cravings in a fraction of a second, it's a good idea to have a plan for how you'll handle these situations before they happen. When Blake and Carlos feel vulnerable, they remind each other why they don't want to use again. Think about a positive goal you want to achieve or another reason why you want to stay sober, such as how happy you are now that your parents trust you again. Remind yourself of a negative consequence of using, such as failing a urine test and getting into trouble at school or with the law.

What if you find yourself at a party where drugs and alcohol are everywhere and kids are hassling you about being sober? Will you walk away? Will you call a friend or family member for a ride? Planning for these scenarios before they happen can help you feel more secure in the moment.

HELP OTHERS

Many people find that helping others is a great way to help themselves. By helping Blake stay sober, Carlos is reinforcing his own goal of sobriety. When you understand how difficult recovery is, you're in a great position to help other people who are also battling addiction.

TREAT OTHER MENTAL HEALTH DISORDERS

As already mentioned, having a mental illness in addition to addiction is common and it's very important to treat both problems. If you've been using alcohol to cope with anxiety, for example, you're going to have a tough time quitting if you're stressed out all the time. To work

PLAN FOR STRESS

Stress is a fact of life and a common cause of relapse, so any plan you make for staying sober will work best if you include ways to cope with stress and anxiety. Identify the main sources of stress in your life. What can you do to change the situation or your reaction to it? Handling issues when they come up, instead of ignoring them, can get rid of little problems before they transform into unmanageable monsters.

THE CHALLENGE OF AVOIDING DRUGS

According to a 2010 survey by the National Center on Addiction and Substance Abuse, 76 percent of teens get their drugs from friends and classmates.[1]

on your mental-health issue, you may need to see a counselor or therapist in addition to continuing with your aftercare program.

IF YOU RELAPSE

Remember that relapse is a part of the disease of addiction, and it doesn't mean you're bad or weak. Whether you backslide a little or return to full-blown abuse, don't be afraid to ask for help. Get support right away so you don't undo all the results you've already achieved.

It helps some people to think of their sobriety one moment at a time. For example, if you can stay sober for the next 60 seconds, and then for the next five minutes, and then for the next half hour, the cravings will diminish. Every day you stay sober adds up until your changed behavior becomes automatic and you're not using anymore. Statistics show that the longer you're sober, the longer you are likely to remain sober.[2]

ASK YOURSELF THIS

- *How easy or difficult would it be for you to get drugs at school? Do you ever feel, like Blake, that you have to "put on mental armor" at school? Why or why not?*

- *Carlos and Blake help each other stay sober. Who in your life do you trust most to help you stay sober?*

- *What kind of sober identity do you imagine for yourself? How do you look? What do you sound like? How do you act?*

- *Is it tough or easy for you to accept help? Think of at least one person who you think would gladly assist you with your sobriety. What will you ask this person to do?*

- *Can you imagine helping someone else with his or her sobriety? What might you do for this person?*

TALK THERAPY FOR ADDICTION

Talk therapy is another term for individual counseling, where you meet with a therapist one-on-one to work on your addiction. Cognitive-behavioral therapy is one approach often used in addiction. The goal in this type of therapy is to change your addiction behavior by changing your thinking. The therapist helps you recognize the thoughts and feelings that led to your substance use, and then he or she teaches you new skills for replacing those old thoughts and behaviors with healthier habits. Clinical studies have shown that cognitive-behavioral therapy is effective in treating addiction.[3]

8

"I'VE GOT THIS FRIEND. . . .": REACHING OUT

Sameena sees Tricia outside the mall restroom. Tricia hasn't been to school all week, and Sam's relieved to see her. From a distance, Tricia looks the same as always—petite and cute. But when Sam gets up

If you think your friend has an addiction, show that you care by talking to her about it and taking steps to get her help if needed.

close, Tricia's eyes seem dull. Her hair sticks out like she didn't comb it this morning.

"Hey," Sam says, concern in her voice. "You okay? You didn't answer my texts."

Tricia shrugs, clenching her jaw.

"Have you been sick or something?"

"No." Tricia's eyes dart down the corridor. "I have to go, okay?"

"Sure." Sam watches as Tricia trots over to Randy and Taylor, the biggest druggies at their high school. Sam's heart sinks. She and Tricia have been friends since first grade. They joined Girl Scouts together and always played on the same soccer teams. But for the past year or so, it's as if Tricia's been slowly self-destructing. She dropped soccer. And she's on academic probation for bad grades.

At first, Sam thought it was depression—Tricia has lots of stuff going on at home. And maybe that's part of the problem. But now she wonders if Tricia's into drugs. Sam takes a deep breath. She's no angel herself. If Tricia needs something now and then to get herself going, is that such a big deal?

Someone grabs Sam's shoulder. "I'm starving! Pizza or Chinese?" It's Jin, Sam's boyfriend. He nudges her toward the food court.

Sam tries to smile but can't. "I'm worried about Tricia. I just saw her with Randy and Taylor."

"Oh, that's not good. They were expelled from school for dealing."

"Dealing! Like what?"

"Weed, coke, meth. If Tricia's hanging out with them, it's not a good sign."

Sam feels sick to her stomach. It looks like her friend is in trouble. But what can she do about it?

RED FLAGS OF SUBSTANCE ABUSE

Having a friend like Tricia who's struggling with addiction can be sad, scary, and confusing. You're concerned and want to help, but where do you start? If you're not certain your friend is abusing alcohol or drugs, here are some warning signs:

- You smell drugs or alcohol on your friend's clothing or breath.

- You've seen your friend with drug supplies (rolling papers, pills, pipe, or a flask, for example).

- Your friend's grades are getting worse; she skips classes and doesn't seem motivated to finish assignments.

- You're aware that your friend isn't sleeping much; maybe she doesn't seem to bathe as often as before and just looks messy.

- Your friend isn't involved in school or extracurricular activities, such as sports or clubs, like he used to be.

- Your friend's moods and behaviors have changed; maybe he's irritable, aggressive, depressed, or talks about suicide.

- Your friend hangs out with gang members or kids who have legal problems.

IF YOU SEE RED FLAGS

First, keep in mind that a change in your friend's mood or behavior doesn't necessarily mean she's abusing alcohol or drugs. Your friend may be depressed or dealing with personal issues you're unaware of. It's still okay to talk to your friend about your concerns, and sooner is better

TALKING TIPS

- Make sure you talk to your friend in a place that's private, but where you feel safe and can leave easily if your friend gets angry. If your friend does get angry, save your talk for another time or ask an adult to help.
- Plan and practice what you're going to say. Talking points might include telling your friend what you've noticed about her recent changes in behavior and that you're concerned. Write down information that you can give your friend, such as hotline phone numbers.
- A calm and caring tone of voice works better than an aggressive or angry tone.
- When you're done talking, listen to what your friend has to say. Discuss what her next step might be.
- Keep the details of your conversation to yourself.

Even if your friend isn't ready to talk, it is important for her to know you are there to listen.

than later. Your friend may need someone to talk to.

Maybe you're hesitating to talk to your friend about drugs because you're worried he'll get mad, or that you'll seem uncool, or that it's none of your business. But think about how you would feel if you were in trouble. Would you want a friend to show he cared about you?

Choose a time when you're sure your friend isn't drunk or high, and openly talk to him or her about your concerns. Let your friend know you're there. Refer your friend to a trusted adult who can help. Your school guidance counselor, a pastor, a favorite teacher, a coach, or a doctor are good choices.

IF YOUR FRIEND IS TRYING TO STAY OFF DRUGS OR ALCOHOL

One of the most important things you can do for a friend who's recovering from addiction is to be available. Your friend may be in the process of switching to a new peer group and trying new activities to avoid the triggers connected with her old lifestyle. She needs friends who are completely supportive and who offer lots of praise and encouragement. Here are a few supportive things you can do:

- Let your friend know he can count on you. This may mean listening to your friend in the middle of the night when he's lonely and struggling with cravings.

- Help keep your friend busy. Invite her along on activities that have nothing to do with

DRUG-FREE FUN

Running out of ideas for what to do with your friend in recovery? Here are a few: Cook or bake, play video or board games, go for a walk or play a sport, go to a local ball game, write in a journal, go to the library, read, plant something in a garden, volunteer at a local food pantry or animal shelter, get involved in a community or church youth group, go for a hike, play musical instruments, ride a bike, go bowling, fly a kite, clean out your closet and donate old clothes, or explore colleges and careers.

drinking or using drugs, such as going to the movies or shopping at the mall.

- Be a good role model. Don't drink or use drugs yourself.

- Agree, if you can, to be a member of your friend's safe-ride team. These are friends and family members who will give your friend a ride out of an unsafe situation, no questions asked.

- Remember that relapse is a symptom of addiction and does not mean your friend is bad or weak. If your friend relapses, remind him that you're still his friend. Talk to your friend openly if you notice that he's backsliding.

- Your friend may not want to accept your help if she's relapsed and is actively using. In that case, it's okay to talk about your friend to an adult you trust, such as your parent or a school counselor. Your goal is to get your friend the help she needs; try not to think of it as sneaking behind your friend's back.

If you've reached out and your friend still abuses substances, don't blame yourself. Addiction is a disease that is very difficult to stop. By being a supportive, nonjudgmental, and sober role model, you're giving your friend more help than you may realize.

ASK YOURSELF THIS

- *Name all of the red flags Sam sees that are clues Tricia may have a drug problem.*

- *If you were Sam, would you talk to Tricia about your concerns? Why or why not?*

- *If you had a friend you thought was addicted, what would you say to start the conversation? What's the next thing you'd say?*

- *Would it be easy or difficult for you to accept an old friend back into your life who's now trying to stay away from drugs or alcohol? Explain your answer.*

- *Do you think it's possible to be a good role model for a friend in recovery if you continue using drugs or alcohol? Why or why not?*

REACHING OUT ON A LARGER SCALE

If you want to help other teens with addictions, check with your school to see if there are programs you can become involved in. Find out if your community participates in anti-drug programs. One national program is Red Ribbon Week, the nation's oldest and largest drug prevention program. Red Ribbon Week is the last week of October each year. For more information, go to the National Family Partnership Web site at www.nfp.org.

9

FROM ABSTINENCE TO USING RESPONSIBLY: PREVENTION

lyssa glances around the room. Mostly old-timers trickle in. Then a minute before the meeting starts, Jenny walks through the door. Her shoulders are slouched, her eyes lowered like she's going to a funeral. Alyssa's heart aches for Jenny, but she smiles

*Find a sponsor or mentor who knows what you are
going through and can help you prevent a relapse.*

and waves from the back row. Jenny plops into
the folding chair next to Alyssa and crosses her
arms.

"Hi," Alyssa says. "I'm glad you could
make it."

At first Jenny doesn't answer. Then she
says, "Is everyone here ancient?"

Alyssa laughs. "Not everyone."

The meeting gets underway. A middle-
aged woman and then a guy in a suit tell their
addiction stories—blackouts, DUIs, broken
marriages, kids' forgotten birthdays. The last
speaker is bald, wrinkled, and hasn't shaved in
a few days. At first Jenny squirms in her seat,
but as the man talks she sits so still, Alyssa can
tell she's paying attention.

The meeting ends. There's a good chance
Jenny will leap up and sprint out the door, so
Alyssa's a little surprised when she doesn't
move. The room empties around them.

"That last guy," Jenny finally says. Her
eyes are wet; she's been crying. "He's older
than my grandfather. But I understood what he
was talking about. It was like he was telling my
story."

"Happens to me all the time," Alyssa says
softly. "Want some coffee? There's a Starbuck's
down the block."

After talking for an hour over coffee, they walk back into the cold afternoon. Alyssa stuffs her hands into her pockets where she feels her three-year sobriety chip. Jenny won't be the first newcomer Alyssa has ever sponsored, or the last. Helping others is the best feeling in the world. "There's a meeting on Saturday that usually has more kids our age," she says. "Want to come?"

Jenny hesitates and then nods.

As they separate at the corner, Alyssa says, "One day at a time, okay?"

Jenny takes a deep breath and smiles. "Yeah. One day at a time. Thanks."

STAYING SOBER

For anyone addicted to drugs or alcohol, staying sober is a minute-by-minute, day-by-day challenge. But for Alyssa, the longer she stays sober, the better she feels about herself, and the less she wants to return to her old lifestyle. That's how it is for a lot of people recovering from addiction—feeling good without alcohol or drugs is a great incentive for staying sober and one of the best forms of prevention.

The goal for anyone in recovery is complete abstinence—not taking the addictive substance at all. Once your brain has been altered by addiction, there is no going back to "social" drinking or "light" using. Addiction is a chronic, lifelong disease.

The one exception to this rule might be if you need a prescription medication to relieve pain, anxiety, or some other ailment. In these cases, your doctor should give you safe doses and closely monitor your use of the drug.

To stay abstinent, you need to avoid high-risk situations and triggers, stick with your treatment plan, and immediately return to treatment if you relapse.

Abstinence is also the surest form of prevention for people who aren't addicted. Even if everyone in your immediate family were dependent on drugs or alcohol and you had several other risk factors for addiction, you'd never become addicted if you never used.

The problem is, the more risk factors you have, the greater the chance that you'll take that first drink or smoke that first joint. The chance

THE COSTS OF ADDICTION

Another reason why prevention is important is the costs associated with addiction. According to the US Department of Health and Human Services,

Substance abuse clearly is among the most costly health problems in the United States. Among national estimates of the costs of illness for 33 diseases and conditions, alcohol ranked second, tobacco ranked sixth, and drug disorders ranked seventh.[1]

FAMILY DINNERS

The National Center on Addiction and Substance Abuse at Columbia University has found that "the more often children have dinner with their parents, the less likely they are to smoke, drink or use drugs." For example, teens who eat fewer than three dinners with their family per week are twice as likely to use tobacco or marijuana and one-and-a-half times more likely to use alcohol. This study also found that listening to each other at the dinner table, instead of texting or watching TV, is a protective factor.[2]

that you'll end up abusing or dependent on a substance is greater also.

PROTECTIVE FACTORS

Just as risk factors make addiction more likely, there are protective factors that make it less likely that you'll use drugs or alcohol. Protective factors show up at home, in schools, and in the community, and drug prevention programs target these three areas.

Protective factors at home include strong bonds between parents and kids, plenty of parental involvement, clear limits, and consistent discipline. Family-oriented prevention programs include parent drug education classes, parenting skills classes, family therapy, home drug testing, and curfews.

Because kids are more likely to use drugs, alcohol, and tobacco products if these

Having a good relationship with your parents or guardians makes you less likely to become addicted, and more likely to recover if you do become addicted.

substances are available in their home, having a drug- and alcohol-free household is another family protective factor.

Students who are academically or socially unsuccessful in school, especially kids who don't feel valued by teachers and friends, are more likely to use drugs and alcohol. That's why school protective factors include focusing on increasing academic skills, self-esteem, self-control, coping strategies, and peer relationships.

School prevention programs include after-school drug education classes, drug testing, teaching kids how to say "no" to peer pressure, and school counseling.

Protective factors in the community include religious groups, law enforcement, government organizations, and the media. To be most successful, prevention on a community scale needs to be consistent and must use the greatest number of places to get the message out. Prevention programs include billboards with drug facts, drug-free zones, and zero-tolerance strategies.

USING RESPONSIBLY

When it comes to addiction, zero tolerance means a policy of abstinence—using no drugs or alcohol whatsoever. While some people argue that zero tolerance is always the best approach to addiction prevention, others say that as long as society gives kids mixed messages about using drugs and alcohol, teens will experiment no matter what rules are in place. The Drug Policy Alliance, for example, has created the Safety First project that promotes drug education, counseling, and open communication instead of zero-tolerance, drug testing, and punishment. They believe the best addiction prevention is about kids being fully informed so they can make good decisions.[3]

A DRUG-FREE FUTURE

Wherever you fall on the addiction spectrum—whether you abuse a substance occasionally or have been dependent on it for some time—you can have a drug-free future. If you can't quit using on your own, get help now to prevent addiction from taking control of your life. Keep your goals for the future close to your heart, and set yourself on a path toward meeting them head-on with a clean body and a clear mind.

PREVENTION PROGRAMS WORK

Whatever your philosophy on prevention, it's a fact that good programs get the job done. The Department of Health and Human Services reports, "If effective prevention programs were implemented nationwide, substance abuse initiation would decline for 1.5 million youth and be delayed for 2 years on average, reducing subsequent problems later in life."[4]

Living with addiction may never be easy, but it doesn't have to keep you from achieving your dreams.

ASK YOURSELF THIS

- *Why do you believe Alyssa thinks helping others is the best feeling in the world? How does this help her stay sober?*

- *Why do you think Alyssa says, "One day at a time," to Jenny? What's your opinion of this philosophy?*

- *What protective factors do you have in your life? Do you think your protective factors outweigh your risk factors, or vice versa?*

- *How many dinners do you eat at home with your family per week? Why do you think spending mealtime with family decreases substance use?*

- *Which prevention policy makes more sense to you—zero tolerance or responsible use? Explain your answer.*

JUST THE FACTS

Addiction is a chronic, relapsing disease of the brain characterized by intense cravings for drugs or alcohol and continued use despite harmful consequences.

Addiction disrupts the chemicals in the brain that balance pleasure seeking with decision making.

Addiction gradually progresses through increasingly severe levels of abuse and dependence.

People who have progressed to substance dependence have both physical and behavioral symptoms.

Risk factors for addiction include genetic makeup, social environment, mental health, the user's age, and the strength and administration of the drug.

The most common serious complication of addiction is injury and death associated with vehicle and other accidents.

Other complications of alcohol and drug addiction include overdose, mental health problems, conflicts with family and friends, and financial and legal problems.

Most people stop using drugs or alcohol on their own before becoming addicted. But once addicted, quitting without treatment can be very difficult.

Recovery from addiction progresses through three phases of treatment: detoxification, rehabilitation, and aftercare.

Detox lasts a few days, or until the drug is out of the body. Each drug has its own withdrawal symptoms.

The main goal of rehabilitation is to learn how to change behavior in order to live drug-free.

Rehab programs take place in full-time residential or part-time outpatient settings. Which setting is best for each person depends on factors such as cost, home environment, and mental health issues.

Aftercare can include support groups, 12-step programs, individual counseling, and alternative therapies. Aftercare provides support while an addict changes to a drug- or alcohol-free lifestyle.

Relapse is a common part of recovery, especially within the first 90 days after rehab treatment ends. Relapse can occur when emotions and physical senses trigger cravings for alcohol or drugs.

Changing to a substance-free lifestyle often means hanging out with friends who don't drink or use substances and getting involved in new activities. Sticking with treatment and planning for triggers also helps with this process.

Abstinence is the best prevention for anyone with a substance addiction. Protective factors help to prevent or delay the initial use of drugs and alcohol.

WHERE TO TURN

If You Think You Might Be Addicted

If you're confused about whether you have an addiction and would like more information, talk to your school counselor or another trusted adult. Check out addiction Web sites for teens such as Above the Influence (www.abovetheinfluence.com), NIDA for Teens (teens.drugabuse.gov), and Teens Health (kidshealth.org/teen/your_mind/problems/addictions.html). If you want to talk to someone right now, call the Girls & Boys Town National Hotline at 1-800-448-3000.

If You Think Your Friend Is Addicted

If you're unsure whether your friend has an addiction problem, compare his or her behavior to "Red Flags for Substance Abuse" in Chapter 8. For more signs of addiction and tips on how to reach out, check out Web sites such as Above the Influence (www.abovetheinfluence.com/help) and Al-Anon/Alateen (www.al-anon.alateen.org/alateen.html). Talk to your school guidance counselor, a pastor, favorite teacher, coach, or doctor. Remember, if you've reached out and your friend still abuses substances, don't blame yourself. Addiction is very difficult to stop.

If You're Having Thoughts of Suicide

Feeling out of control with alcohol or drugs can create a sense of helplessness and hopelessness. If you're already depressed or lonely, using substances can make your anxiety or depression worse. If you've had thoughts of suicide, please get help right away from your doctor, school counselor, school nurse, teacher, relative, or other trusted adult. You can also call the National Suicide Prevention Lifeline at 1-800-273-TALK (1-800-273-8255), the USA National Suicide Hotline at 1-800-SUICIDE (1-800-784-2433), or the Girls & Boys Town National Hotline (1-800-448-3000), 24 hours a day, seven days a week.

If You're Wondering Where to Find an Addiction Specialist or Treatment Program

Your family doctor, school nurse, or school counselor may be able to recommend an addiction specialist, or you can check online for board-certified doctors with addiction experience at the American Society of Addiction Medicine (www.asam.org) or the American Academy of Addiction Psychiatry (www.aaap.org).

Teen addiction is different from adult addiction, so if you can, it's important to choose a rehab program designed for adolescents. To find teen rehab programs, check out Choose Help (www.choosehelp.com/rehab-programs/teen-rehab or 1-877-830-7020) or Drug Strategies (www.drugstrategies.org or 1-800-559-9503). To find community-based addiction services, you can contact the Center for Substance Abuse Treatment (www.csat.samhsa.gov or 1-800-662-4357). And for free treatment centers, try www.soberrecovery.com.

If Your Parents Use Drugs or Alcohol

If your mom or dad abuses drugs or alcohol, you're not alone. It's important to remember that it's not your fault your parents use drugs or alcohol, and you can't make them stop. But you can get more information and help for yourself. Talk to a trusted adult, such as your school counselor. You can also check out organizations such as the National Association for Children of Alcoholics (www.nacoa.org/cankids.htm), the Children of Alcoholics Foundation (www.coaf.org or 1-800-359-COAF), or Alateen (www.alateen.org). Or call the NineLine at 1-800-999-9999 for help 24 hours a day, seven days a week. Your parents can get help by contacting the National Clearinghouse for Alcohol and Drug Information at 1-800-729-6686.

GLOSSARY

abstinence
The practice of not using alcohol or drugs.

aftercare
The care and treatment given to persons discharged from an institution.

chronic
Lasting a long time.

co-occurring disorders
When both a substance use disorder and a mental disorder are present at the same time; also called comorbidity.

depressant
The category of drugs that reduce anxiety and cause sleepiness; includes alcohol, barbiturates, and benzodiazepines.

detoxification
The period during which an addictive substance is not taken and completely leaves the body; also called detox.

dopamine
A brain chemical that is involved in feeling pleasure.

euphoria
The feeling of intense pleasure that may be temporarily experienced after using a substance.

hallucinogen
A category of drugs that alter perceptions; includes LSD, mescaline, Ecstasy, PCP, and psilocybin.

opiate
A category of drugs derived from the opium plant; includes heroin, opium, codeine, oxycodone (OxyContin), and Vicodin.

overdose
A dose of drugs or alcohol large enough to cause death.

prefrontal cortex
The area of the brain involved in decision making, which is located behind the forehead.

psychoactive
Having an effect on the mind.

rehabilitation
Substance abuse treatment programs; can take place in outpatient or inpatient settings; also called rehab.

relapse
When a person returns to drinking or taking drugs after a period of not using.

stimulant
A category of drugs that elevate the mood and increase alertness; includes cocaine, methamphetamine, and Ritalin.

trigger
A physical or emotional cue that causes cravings for drugs or alcohol.

withdrawal
The physical effects that occur when a person suddenly stops taking an addictive substance.

ADDITIONAL RESOURCES

SELECTED BIBLIOGRAPHY

Aue, Pamela Willwerth, ed. *Teen Drug Abuse*. Detroit: Thomson/Gale, 2006. Print.

Coombs, Robert H. *Handbook of Addictive Disorders: A Practical Guide to Diagnosis and Treatment*. Hoboken, NJ: Wiley, 2004. Print.

"Drug Addiction." *Mayo Clinic*. Mayo Clinic, 2 Oct. 2009. Web. 23 May 2011.

Hoffman, John, and Susan Froemke, eds. *Addiction: Why Can't They Just Stop?* New York: Rodale, 2007. Print.

National Clearinghouse for Alcohol and Drug Information. Web. 23 May 2011.

National Institute on Drug Abuse. *Drugs, Brains, and Behavior: The Science of Addiction*. NIH Pub No. 10-5605, Aug. 2010. PDF file.

Results from the 2009 National Survey on Drug Use and Health: Volume I. Summary of National Findings. Rockville, MD: Substance Abuse and Mental Health Services Administration, 2010. PDF file.

FURTHER READINGS

KidsPeace. *I've Got This Friend Who: Advice for Teens and Their Friends on Alcohol, Drugs, Eating Disorder, Risky Behavior and More*. Center City, MN: Hazelden Publishing, 2007. Print.

Kuhn, Cynthia, Scott Swartzwelder, and Wilkie Wilson. *Buzzed: The Straight Facts About the Most Used and Abused Drugs from Alcohol to Ecstasy*. 3rd ed. New York: Norton, 2008. Print.

Less, Nicholas R., and Sara Dulaney Gilbert. *Living with Alcoholism and Drug Addiction (Teen's Guides)*. New York: Checkmark, 2009. Print.

WEB LINKS

To learn more about living with substance addiction, visit ABDO Publishing Company online at **www.abdopublishing.com**. Web sites about living with substance addiction are featured on our Book Links page. These links are routinely monitored and updated to provide the most current information available.

SOURCE NOTES

CHAPTER 1: WHAT IS ADDICTION? SYMPTOMS AND DEFINITIONS

1. *Results from the 2009 National Survey on Drug Use and Health: Volume I. Summary of National Findings.* Rockville, MD: Substance Abuse and Mental Health Services Administration, 2010. PDF file.

2. Michael B. First, Allen Frances, and Harold Alan Pincus. *DSM-IV-TR Guidebook.* Arlington, VA: American Psychiatric Association, 2004. Print. 128, 133.

3. *Results from the 2009 National Survey on Drug Use and Health: Volume I. Summary of National Findings.* Rockville, MD: Substance Abuse and Mental Health Services Administration, 2010. PDF file.

4. John Hoffman and Susan Froemke, eds. *Addiction: Why Can't They Just Stop?* New York: Rodale, 2007. Print. 99, 101.

5. *Results from the 2009 National Survey on Drug Use and Health: Volume I. Summary of National Findings.* Rockville, MD: Substance Abuse and Mental Health Services Administration, 2010. PDF file.

6. "Tobacco Use by Young People." *Centers for Disease Control and Prevention.* Centers for Disease Control and Prevention, 2010. Web. 3 May 2011.

CHAPTER 2: IT'S NOT JUST ABOUT WILLPOWER: CAUSES AND RISK FACTORS

1. John Hoffman and Susan Froemke, eds. *Addiction: Why Can't They Just Stop?* New York: Rodale, 2007. Print. 34.

2. James D. Stoehr. *The Neurobiology of Addiction.* Philadelphia: Chelsea House, 2006. Print. 67.

3. Ibid.

4. "Fact Sheet: Alcohol Advertising and Youth." *The Center on Alcohol Marketing and Youth.* The Center on Alcohol Marketing and Youth. Apr. 2007. Web. 24 Nov. 2010.

5. Meg Riordan. "Tobacco Company Marketing to Kids." *Campaign for Tobacco Free Kids.* Campaign for Tobacco Free Kids, 20 July 2010. Web. 3 Dec. 2010.

6. John Hoffman and Susan Froemke, eds. *Addiction: Why Can't They Just Stop?* New York: Rodale, 2007. Print. 97.

7. *Results from the 2009 National Survey on Drug Use and Health: Volume I. Summary of National Findings.* Rockville, MD: Substance Abuse and Mental Health Services Administration, 2010. PDF file.

8. John Hoffman and Susan Froemke, eds. *Addiction: Why Can't They Just Stop?* New York: Rodale, 2007. Print. 96.

CHAPTER 3: SOBERING FACTS: COMPLICATIONS OF ADDICTION

1. "For Teens: So what's the big deal, anyway?" *Center for Adolescent Substance Abuse Research.* Center for Adolescent Substance Abuse Research, 2009. Web. 1 Dec. 2010.

2. Louise I. Gerdes, ed. *Addiction, Opposing Viewpoints.* Farmington Hills, MI: Greenhaven, 2005. Print. 73.

3. "For Teens: So what's the big deal, anyway?" *Center for Adolescent Substance Abuse Research.* Center for Adolescent Substance Abuse Research, 2009. Web. 1 Dec. 2010.

4. "Underage Drinking Has Serious Consequences." *Substance Abuse and Mental Health Services Administration.* Substance Abuse and Mental Health Services Administration, n.d. Web. 12 Dec. 2010.

5. John Hoffman and Susan Froemke, eds. *Addiction: Why Can't They Just Stop?* New York: Rodale, 2007. Print. 98.

6. "Frequent Consumption of Energy Drinks is Associated with Problematic Alcohol Consumption." *Treatment Research Institute.* Treatment Research Institute, 18 Nov. 2010. Web. 5 Dec. 2010.

7. *The Surgeon General's Call to Action to Prevent and Reduce Underage Drinking.* Rockville, MD: U.S. Department of Health and Human Services, 2007. PDF file.

CHAPTER 4: TREATMENT, PART I: GETTING HELP AND DETOX

1. *Results from the 2009 National Survey on Drug Use and Health: Volume I. Summary of National Findings.* Rockville, MD: Substance Abuse and Mental Health Services Administration, 2010. PDF file.

2. Ibid.

3. John Hoffman and Susan Froemke, eds. *Addiction: Why Can't They Just Stop?* New York: Rodale, 2007. Print. 100.

SOURCE NOTES CONTINUED

4. "Drug Addiction: Treatment and Drugs." *Mayo Clinic*. Mayo Clinic, 2 Oct. 2009. Web. 20 Nov. 2010.

5. Ibid.

6. Ibid.

7. Ibid.

8. Ibid.

9. "Understanding Nicotine Withdrawal—Symptoms." *WebMD*. WebMD, 6 Dec. 2009. Web. 9 Dec. 2010.

CHAPTER 5: TREATMENT, PART II: REHAB

1. *Under the Counter: The Diversion and Abuse of Controlled Prescription Drugs in the US. National Center on Addiction and Substance Abuse at Columbia University*. New York: The National Center on Addiction and Substance Abuse at Columbia University, July 2005. PDF file.

2. John Hoffman and Susan Froemke, eds. *Addiction: Why Can't They Just Stop?* New York: Rodale, Inc., 2007. Print. 109.

3. Ibid.

4. "Dual Diagnosis: Adolescents with Co-occurring Brain Disorders & Substance Abuse Disorders." *National Alliance on Mental Illness*. National Alliance on Mental Illness. 2 Jan. 2011. Web. 23 May 2011.

5. "Tobacco Use by Young People." *Centers for Disease Control and Prevention*. Centers for Disease Control and Prevention, 2010. Web. 3 May 2011.

CHAPTER 6: AFTERCARE, TRIGGERS, AND RELAPSE: RECOVERY

1. John Hoffman and Susan Froemke, eds. *Addiction: Why Can't They Just Stop?* New York: Rodale, 2007. Print. 115.

2. AA Grapevine. *Young People and AA*. New York: Alcoholics Anonymous World Services, 2007. PDF file.

3. Louise I. Gerdes, ed. *Addiction, Opposing Viewpoints*. Farmington Hills, MI: Greehaven, 2005. Print. 94.

4. Robert H. Coombs. *Handbook of Addictive Disorders: A Practical Guide to Diagnosis and Treatment*. Hoboken, NJ: John Wiley & Sons, 2004. Print. 116–117.

5. John Hoffman and Susan Froemke, eds. *Addiction: Why Can't They Just Stop?* New York: Rodale, 2007. Print. 107.

CHAPTER 7: A SOBER LIFESTYLE: COPING WITH ADDICTION

1. *National Survey of American Attitudes on Substance Abuse XV: Teens and Parents.* New York: The National Center on Addiction and Substance Abuse at Columbia University, Aug. 2010. PDF file.

2. John Hoffman and Susan Froemke, eds. *Addiction: Why Can't They Just Stop?* New York: Rodale, 2007. Print. 222.

3. Robert H. Coombs. *Handbook of Addictive Disorders: A Practical Guide to Diagnosis and Treatment.* Hoboken, NJ: John Wiley & Sons, 2004. Print. 113.

CHAPTER 8: "I'VE GOT THIS FRIEND. . . .": REACHING OUT

None.

CHAPTER 9: FROM ABSTINENCE TO USING RESPONSIBLY: PREVENTION

1. T. Miller and D. Hendrie. *Substance Abuse Prevention Dollars and Cents: A Cost-Benefit Analysis.* Rockville, MD: Center for Substance Abuse Prevention, Substance Abuse and Mental Health Services Administration, 2008. Print. 1.

2. *The Importance of Family Dinners V. National Center on Addiction and Substance Abuse at Columbia University.* New York: The National Center on Addiction and Substance Abuse at Columbia University, 2009. PDF file.

3. Marsha Rosenbaum. *Safety First: A reality-based approach to teens and drugs.* San Francisco, CA: Drug Policy Alliance, 2007. PDF file.

4. T. Miller and D. Hendrie. *Substance Abuse Prevention Dollars and Cents: A Cost-Benefit Analysis.* Rockville, MD: Center for Substance Abuse Prevention, Substance Abuse and Mental Health Services Administration, 2008. Print.1.

INDEX

ABOUT THE AUTHOR

In addition to writing nonfiction and fiction for children, Melissa Higgins has been a mental health counselor in private practice and in elementary and secondary schools where she's worked with kids, teens, and adults coping with issues including substance abuse. Her books for young readers help them deal with divorce and other family issues.

PHOTO CREDITS